The Uncanny Can

Library of Congress Cataloging-in-Publication Data

Mecozzi, Maureen.
  The Uncanny can / by Maureen Mecozzi.
      p. cm. -- (Shockwave)
  Includes index.
  ISBN 10: 0-531-17584-7 (lib. bdg.)
  ISBN 13: 978-0-531-17584-2 (lib. bdg.)
  ISBN 10: 0-531-18815-9 (pbk.)
  ISBN 13: 978-0-531-18815-6 (pbk.)
1. Canning and preserving--History--Juvenile literature.
2. Food--Preservation--History--Juvenile literature.
I. Title. II. Series.

  TP371.3.M43 2008
  664'.0282--dc22

2007012230

Published in 2008 by Children's Press, an imprint of Scholastic Inc.,
557 Broadway, New York, New York 10012
www.scholastic.com

08 09 10 11 12 13 14 15 16 17
10 9 8 7 6 5 4 3 2 1

Printed in China through Colorcraft Ltd., Hong Kong

Author: Maureen Mecozzi
Educational Consultant: Ian Morrison
Editor: Karen Alexander
Designer: Amy Lam
Photo Researchers: Jamshed Mistry and Sarah Matthewson
Illustrator: Ellen Giggenbach (p. 12)

Photographs by: Alamy: © Sheldon Lewis (p. 3); © Thomas Hallstein (early cans,
pp. 26–27); © The Print Collector (trade cards, p. 27); **Amy Lam** (p. 30); **Aurora Photos:**
Susana Raab (soldier, p. 15); **Big Stock Photo** (can opener, p. 5; warship, car, p. 25);
Courtesy of Ken Stutt (Del Monte canister, p. 31); **Eric Witty** (Pretzels canister, p. 31);
Getty Images (pp. 7–9; p. 14); **Heinz Wattie's Ltd.** by permission (p. 23); **Jennifer and Brian
Lupton** (teenagers, pp. 32–33); **More Images/Nature Picture Library** (p. 11); **Photolibrary**
(p. 10; p. 13; p. 16; pp. 18–19; p. 21); **Stock.Xchng** (film can and clapper board, p. 25);
Stockxpert (can, p. 3, p. 19; trash can, can of worms, p. 25;); **Tranz:** Corbis (cover; p. 12;
food supplies, Scott's hut, p. 17; p. 20; p. 22; p. 28; Campbell's soup can, p. 31; garbage
trucks, pp. 32–33); Popperfoto (Robert Scott, p. 17); **V&A Images/Victoria and Albert
Museum** (windmill and tea caddy, p. 31); **www.stockcentral.co.nz** (p. 29)

The publisher would like to thank Heinz Wattie's Ltd., New Zealand, for the photo of the
production line on page 23, Benjamin Witty for providing the plane model for page 30,
and Amber Jay for providing the pretzels canister on page 31.

All illustrations and other photographs © Weldon Owen Education Inc.

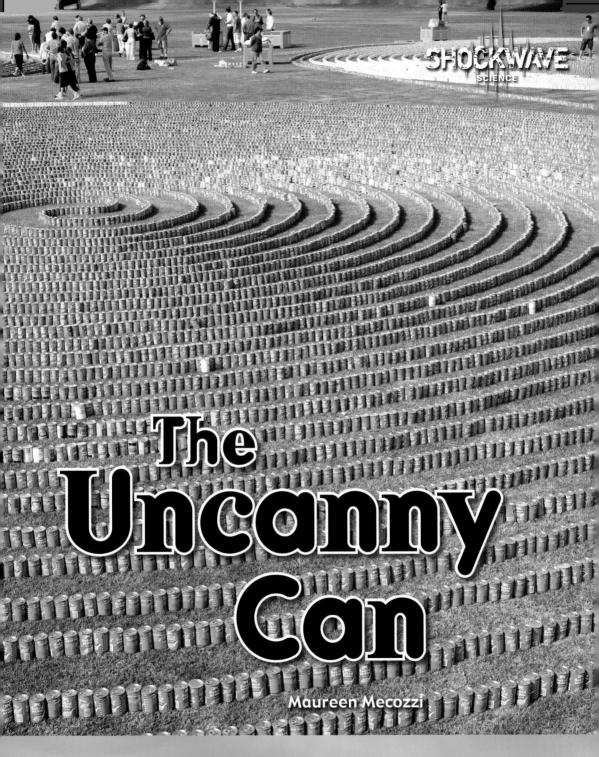

SHOCKWAVE
SCIENCE

The Uncanny Can

Maureen Mecozzi

children's press®

An imprint of Scholastic Inc.

NEW YORK • TORONTO • LONDON • AUCKLAND • SYDNEY
MEXICO CITY • NEW DELHI • HONG KONG
DANBURY, CONNECTICUT

CHECK THESE OUT!

SHOCKER

Stuff to Shock,
Surprise, and
Amaze You

Quick Recaps
and Notable
Notes

Word Stunners
and Other Oddities

The Heads-Up
on Expert Reading

Links to More
Information

CONTENTS

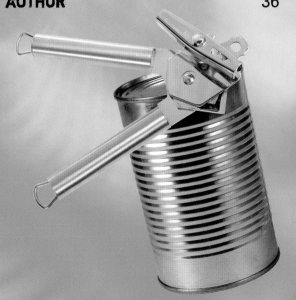

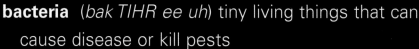

bacteria (*bak TIHR ee uh*) tiny living things that can cause disease or kill pests

cylinder (*SIL uhn dur*) a shape with flat, round ends and sides like a tube, such as a soda can

dehydrator (*dee HYE dray tor*) a machine that dries food

microorganism (*mye kroh OR guh niz uhm*) a tiny living thing that cannot be seen without a microscope. Bacteria are microorganisms.

preserve to prepare food in a way that will prevent it from spoiling

smith a person who works with metal

solder (*SOD ur*) to join pieces of metal together with melted metal

• •

For additional vocabulary, see Glossary on page 34.

Bacteria is the plural of *bacterium*. Other nouns that form their plural in this way include:
curriculum – curricula;
medium – media;
memorandum – memoranda.

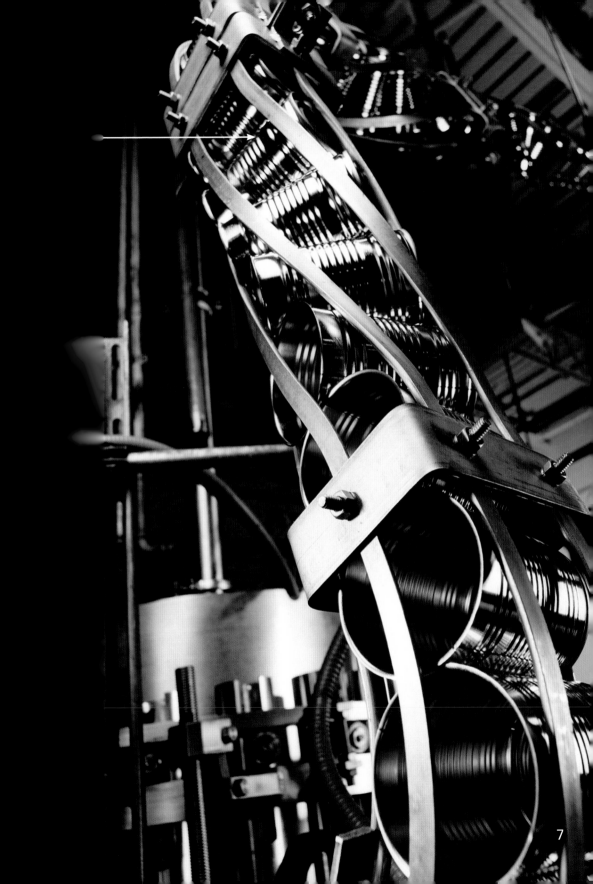

The word *can* is short for "canister."
The first metal containers used
for holding food were called
tin canisters.

Cans come in all shapes
and sizes. Some are
even made to look
like houses and cars.
Cans are used to store
all kinds of things. They
store paint. They store
cough drops. They even
store nuclear waste.

Many of the cans
in this book are used
for food. However, they
do not only store food.
Canning is a way
of **preserving** food.
When food is canned,
it is heated to a very
high temperature.
The heat kills any harmful
bacteria. The food
is then sealed in
an airtight container.

Canned food does not always come in a can. The first canned food was packed in glass jars. Today, canned food is often in a plastic or cardboard pack.

Firsts for Cans

	1810	Tin-plated iron cans used for food
	1812	Canning factory
	1849	Canning machine
	1858	Can opener
	1880s	Automatic can-making machine
	1914	Multicolored cans
	1930s	Canned soda
	1957	Aluminum cans
	1959	Pull-tab cans
	1985	Canned soda taken into outer space
	1997	Ends on cans colored to match rest of can

After early humans killed a woolly mammoth and ate their fill of meat, they had a problem. They needed a way to keep the leftovers! **Microorganisms** can rot food in days if the food is not preserved. Many of the food preservation methods we use today date back to those ancient times.

When there is no moisture in food, the organisms that cause it to rot or grow **mold** cannot live. In hot, dry countries, food can be dried in the sun. Today, a machine called a **dehydrator** is often used to dry food.

Canny is an old English word that means "knowing" or "steady." The word *uncanny* is no longer the opposite of *canny*. Now it means "weird" or "strange."

Woolly mammoths were very large animals.

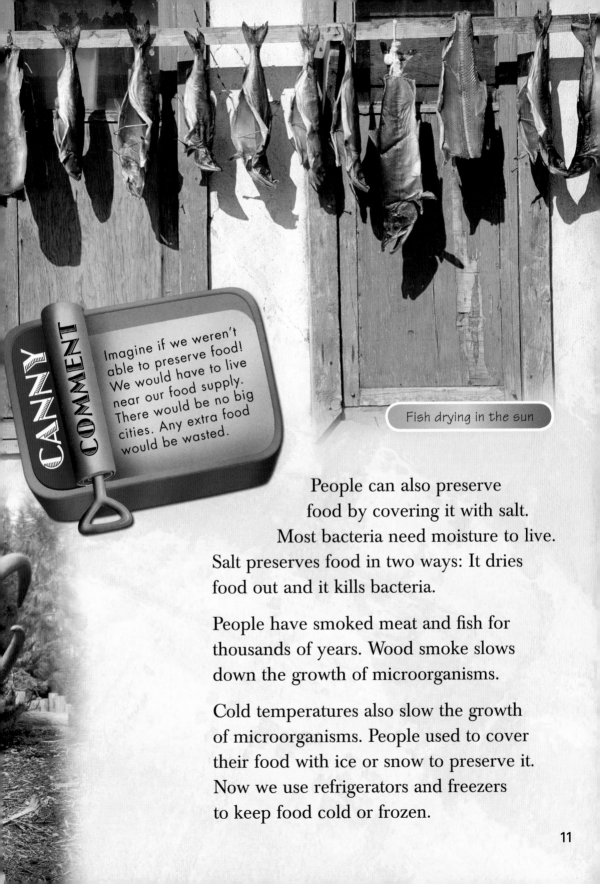

CANNY COMMENT

Imagine if we weren't able to preserve food! We would have to live near our food supply. There would be no big cities. Any extra food would be wasted.

Fish drying in the sun

People can also preserve food by covering it with salt. Most bacteria need moisture to live. Salt preserves food in two ways: It dries food out and it kills bacteria.

People have smoked meat and fish for thousands of years. Wood smoke slows down the growth of microorganisms.

Cold temperatures also slow the growth of microorganisms. People used to cover their food with ice or snow to preserve it. Now we use refrigerators and freezers to keep food cold or frozen.

Napoleon Bonaparte and his army

French emperor Napoleon Bonaparte said, "An army marches on its stomach." He meant that soldiers need good food if they are to be strong enough to win battles. In 1795, he offered a prize to anyone who could get food to the army without it spoiling.

In 1809, a French cook, Nicolas Appert, won the prize. Appert put food in glass jars. He sealed the jars with a cork. Then he heated the jars in boiling water. It worked! The food did not spoil.

There was a problem though. It was difficult to transport glass jars. In 1810, British inventors came up with a new idea. They packed food in cans. In 1815, the British troops faced Napoleon's army at the Battle of Waterloo. By that time, both armies were eating canned food.

When I first read "An army marches on its stomach," it sounded strange. But as I continued to read, it made more sense. It is just an interesting way of saying that armies need to be well fed in order to fight.

SHOCKER

The can opener wasn't invented until 1858. Before that, people had to use a hammer and chisel, or smash the can open with a rock!

Louis Pasteur

Nobody knew why heating food preserved it. Even Nicolas Appert didn't know why his method worked. Then, in 1864, a French chemist, Louis Pasteur, discovered that heat kills the harmful microorganisms in food.

Canned food became an important part of military **rations**. During the American Civil War (1861–1865), soldiers drank milk and ate pork and beans from cans. In World War I, British soldiers survived on cans of corned beef.

During World War II, troops ate 100 million pounds of canned meat. American troops had C rations (canned field rations). Each pack contained a can of meat and vegetables and a canned dessert. It also had a can opener and some extra rations, such as candy.

During World War II, people collected used cans. The cans were melted down to make airplanes and other machines.

SHOCKER

In 1852, the British Navy bought thousands of cans of meat. When the sailors opened the cans, they found the meat had spoiled. Not only was the meat bad, but it included chunks of animal throats and tongues!

CANNY COMMENT

In World War II, a self-heating can was invented. When the wick was lit, it heated an element in the center of the can. The element then heated the food.

Today, the rations for most soldiers are MREs. This means "meals ready to eat." Each pouch comes with a flameless heater. Add water and whoosh! A chemical reaction heats up the food. Soldiers say the food tastes good. The packs are strong enough not to burst if they are dropped from 100 feet.

Did You Know?

Spam™ is ham in a can. It became popular during World War II. In England, there was a shortage of meat. Sometimes Spam™ was the only meat families ate for weeks. At times, American soldiers had to eat Spam™ three times a day!

In America, the demand for canned food rose as settlers moved west in the mid-1800s.

Early explorers and settlers risked **starvation**. Sometimes the food they took with them went bad. Often it wasn't **nutritious** enough to keep them healthy. Settlers took seeds with them to plant where they settled. Often they had no other food supply. If the plants didn't grow, they could starve.

Nicolas Appert had started a process that **revolutionized** the world of food. His canned food was nutritious. It would keep for a long time. It tasted much better than other kinds of preserved food.

SHOCKER

Sir William Parry took canned food on his two Arctic voyages in the 1820s. A can of veal, carried on both trips but never used, was finally opened in 1938. The meat was fed to a cat. The cat survived!

Now explorers and settlers could take a **reliable** food supply to the most remote places in the world. In 1910, British explorer Robert Scott led an **expedition** to the South Pole. Some of the canned food he took with him is still in his supply hut at Cape Evans, in Antarctica. Tragically, the members of the expedition all died of cold and hunger on their way back to the hut.

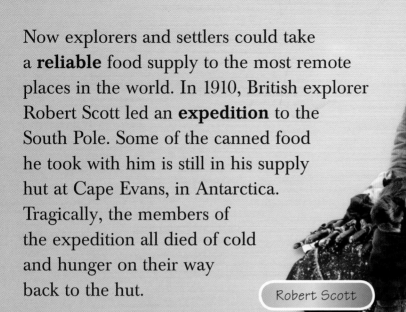

Robert Scott

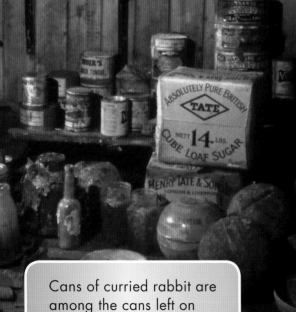

Cans of curried rabbit are among the cans left on

Before canned food:
- food often went bad
- preserved food wasn't very nutritious
- people relied on crops growing well

Canned food:
- was more nutritious
- tasted better
- lasted longer

The first cans were made in the early 1800s. They were made by hand from iron or steel. Steel is a mixture of iron and carbon. **Smiths** pounded the metal into a flat sheet. The sheet was dipped in melted tin to stop it from rusting. Then it was cut and bent around a **cylinder**. The seams and ends were **soldered** with lead. A good smith could make ten cans in a day.

Can-making machines were invented in the mid-1800s. They could make 60 cans in an hour. Today's machines can make 2,500 cans in a minute!

Smiths in an iron workshop in the 1800s

Workers check cans as they come off a production line.

The rings around a can are called beading. Beading makes cans strong. Because beaded cans are stronger than plain cans, they can be thinner. Less metal is needed to make them. They are also lighter.

CANNY COMMENT

Ermal Cleon Fraze of Ohio invented the pull-tab can in 1959. It meant that people who bought soda in a can didn't need a can opener.

The first aluminum cans were made in 1957. Aluminum cans are lighter than steel ones, so they are easier to transport. Aluminum withstands the pressure of fizzy drinks well. It does not rust. It can also be **recycled** easily.

Many canning factories were set up in the mid-1800s. They were close to farming communities. When there were good harvests, the **surplus** fruits and vegetables were canned. Today, many crops are grown specifically for canning.

Shakers, air blasters, and water sprayers remove dirt from the raw produce. Machines shuck corn and pit cherries. They even peel and slice vegetables and fruit.

CANNY COMMENT

Fresh food contains nutrients that keep us healthy. Canned food is **processed** right after the food is harvested. Therefore it keeps its nutrients.

Pineapples being washed

SHOCKER

In the early days of canning, a can of turkey was heated too much. The can exploded. It killed the cook.

Cooked beets being canned

Filling machines pack the food into cans. It is important not to put too much food in the can. If there is too much, the can may burst when it is processed. That is because most food expands when it is heated. When the can is filled, most of the oxygen is removed.

The cans are sealed and heated to a high temperature. Bacteria grow if the food isn't heated for long enough at a high enough temperature. The cans are then cooled in cold water. They are washed. Finally, they are dried with hot air. If a label is needed, a machine sticks it on at this point. Often, though, the label is printed on the can as the can is made.

The filled cans will be sealed. Then they are heated in a large oven.

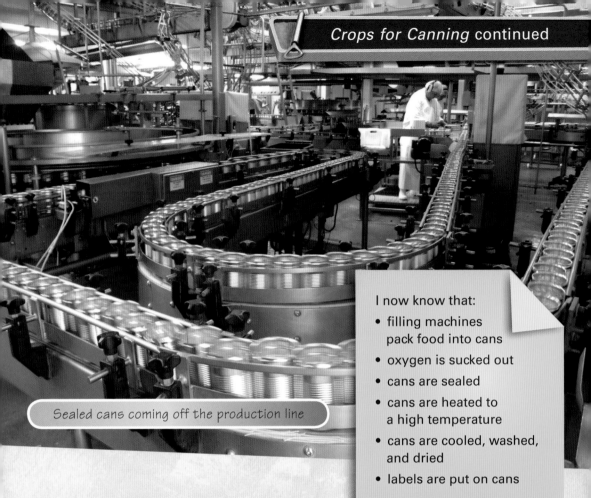

Sealed cans coming off the production line

I now know that:
- filling machines pack food into cans
- oxygen is sucked out
- cans are sealed
- cans are heated to a high temperature
- cans are cooled, washed, and dried
- labels are put on cans

In the past, cans were sealed with lead. Lead is toxic to humans. Sometimes the lead leaked into the insides of the cans. People got ill from eating the food.

Today, machines **crimp** the edges of the lid and the can together to seal the can. Non-toxic coatings cover the seams. Cans for high-acid foods, such as tomatoes, are coated inside. This prevents contact between the food and the metal.

SHOCKER

In 1845, Sir John Franklin led an expedition to find the **Northwest Passage**. He took canned food with him. Lead from the seams of the cans leaked into the food. The food spoiled. The explorers got lead poisoning and food poisoning! They all died.

23

You can learn a lot about a can if you can understand the codes. Each cannery has its own special code. The code tells when the can was processed.

Cannery codes can be hard to figure out. Look at this code: 8195. You'd never know that the numbers mean July 14, 2008: 8 = 2008; 195 = July 14, which is the 195th day of the year.

Canneries also mark their cans so that people know how long they should be kept. "Best by" or "Best before" means that after that date the quality of the food will decline. The "Sell by" or "Pull" date tells the store how long it can keep the can on its shelves.

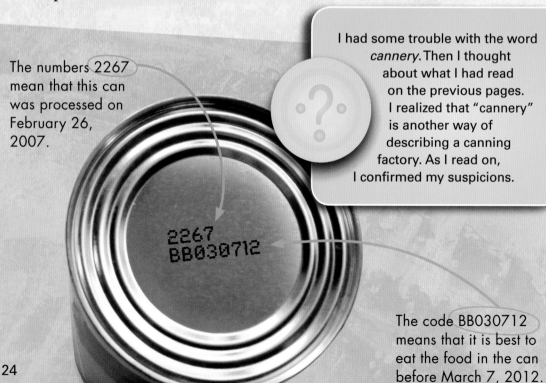

The numbers 2267 mean that this can was processed on February 26, 2007.

I had some trouble with the word *cannery*. Then I thought about what I had read on the previous pages. I realized that "cannery" is another way of describing a canning factory. As I read on, I confirmed my suspicions.

2267
BB030712

The code BB030712 means that it is best to eat the food in the can before March 7, 2012.

Canny Sayings

SHOCKER

Don't open a leaking or bulging can! Bacterial **spores** may be growing inside it. The spores produce a **toxin** that can **paralyze** and kill. The spores can survive being boiled for several hours. If canned food is not processed properly, the spores can multiply and release the poison.

If you have opened up a can of worms, something is much more complicated than you thought it would be.

Canned music is recorded music. At first, music was recorded on cylinders. The cylinders looked like cans.

When a film is "in the can," the director has finished filming it.

A destroyer is sometimes called a tin can or even just a can.

To can an idea or a suggestion means to discard it or throw it out.

Canny Custom

In the Middle Ages, people banged pans and rang bells at a wedding. They did it to frighten away evil spirits. Today, we tie cans to the newlyweds' car.

As long as people have had goods to sell, they have advertised. Food producers are no exception. Canneries began to paste paper labels onto cans in the 1880s. The labels showed what was in the cans. Then packaging changed. The pictures often had nothing to do with what was in the can. They were intended to get people to buy. The colorful cans looked good in the stores too.

Canneries also used to print **trade cards** to persuade people to buy their cans. Children liked to collect the cards. They swapped them with their friends and family members.

Some of these old cans show what is inside the can. Others have pictures designed to appeal to shoppers.

At present, scientists are developing a plastic screen that can be wrapped around cans. It will flash information about special offers and recipes as shoppers walk past.

FAIRBANK CANNING CO.
CHICAGO. ILL.
COOKED CORNED BEEF

THE LION BRAND.

Trade cards

NAPOLÉON I.

VÉRITABLE EXTRAIT DE VIANDE LIEBIG.

ÉPISODES DE L'HISTOIRE DE BELGIQUE (XVIᵉ–XIXᵉ SIÈCLE).
Le corps hollando-belge à la bataille de Waterloo (18 Juin 1815).

Some canneries produced educational trade cards. This one is from the late 1800s. It shows Napoleon and the Battle of Waterloo.

YELLOW CLING PEACHES
NET WEIGHT 1 LB. 4 OZ.

ODY GO BRAND

27

THE THREE R's

Our planet is filling up with trash! Nearly everything we buy comes in packaging. Every day, we add more trash to **landfills**. Steel or aluminum packaging is better than plastic. It can be melted down and reshaped over and over.

Remember the three R's:

- Reduce – use less so that you will throw less away.

- Reuse – use things again.

- Recycle – use old things to make new things.

I already know something about the three R's. I saw a television program about them. It sure makes reading easier when you can make a connection like that.

Aluminum cans are 100 percent recyclable.

Steel

- About 62 percent of the steel used in the United States is recycled.

- More than 600 steel cans are recycled every second.

- It takes 45 seconds to shred a car into fist-sized pieces of steel for recycling.

- Recycling one pound of steel saves enough energy to power a 60-watt lightbulb for 26 hours.

Aluminum

- Aluminum can be recycled quickly. In one year, you could buy four different cans made from the same aluminum.

- Making just one can from recycled aluminum saves enough energy to power a TV for three hours.

- One ton of recycled aluminum saves enough energy to drive a car for 44,000 miles.

Bales of crushed aluminum cans

You don't have to put all your empty cans out with the recycling. There are other ways to recycle them. Many people collect cans. They often like old cans best. Some people enjoy making new things from used cans. They make all kinds of things, such as jewelry and musical instruments. Some people use soda cans to make model cars, ships, and airplanes.

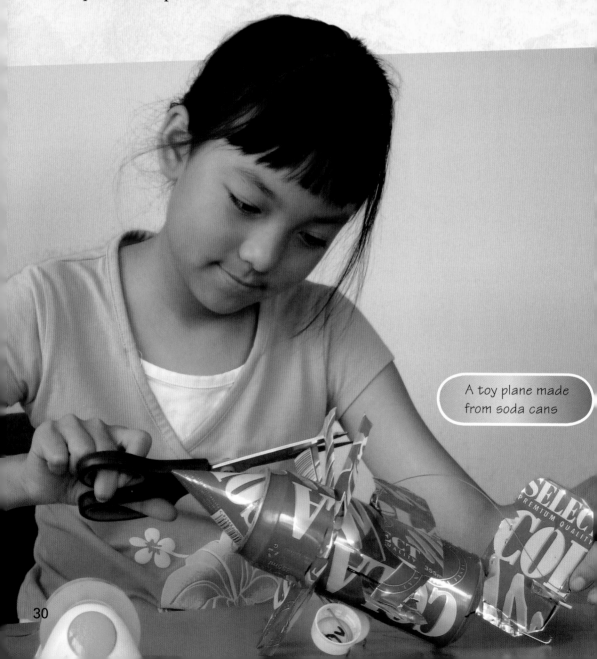

A toy plane made from soda cans

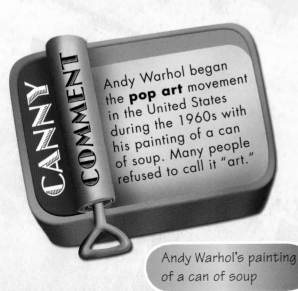

Canisters come in many shapes. The windmill and the Indian canister once held cookies.

CANNY COMMENT

Andy Warhol began the **pop art** movement in the United States during the 1960s with his painting of a can of soup. Many people refused to call it "art."

Andy Warhol's painting of a can of soup

31

An **ecological** footprint is the amount of land and water people use up as they live their lives. People in developed countries have a big ecological footprint. People in less developed countries have a smaller footprint. That is because they use fewer natural resources.

Your ecological footprint relates to more than just the food, water, and energy you use.

WHAT DO YOU THINK?

Do you think we use too much packaging? Should we use less so that we don't create so much trash?

PRO

We use too much packaging. Most packaging is just to make the item look good so that we will buy it. Some things come in layers of packaging. The item is in a bag, which is in a box. The box is then shrink-wrapped. All that packaging adds to the trash in landfills.

It also relates to the amount of trash you create.

Developed countries produce mountains of trash. Much of it is packaging, such as cans. Most of the things we buy come in packages. Many people believe that we should use less packaging. They say packaging is wasteful.

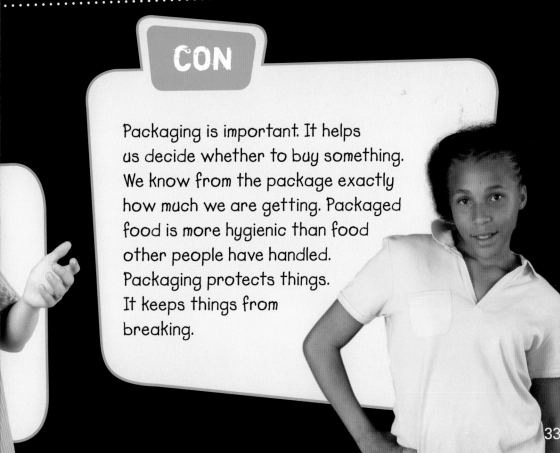

CON

Packaging is important. It helps us decide whether to buy something. We know from the package exactly how much we are getting. Packaged food is more hygienic than food other people have handled. Packaging protects things. It keeps things from breaking.

GLOSSARY

crimp (*KRIMP*) to pinch or press two edges together to form a seal

ecological (*ek uh LOJ i kuhl*) relating to the relationship between living things and their environment

expedition (*ek spuh DISH uhn*) a long journey undertaken by a group with a specific goal

landfill the land where trash is dumped and buried between layers of soil

mold a fungus that grows on food and damp things

Northwest Passage a sea route through the Canadian Arctic, linking the Atlantic Ocean and the Pacific Ocean

nutritious (*noo TRISH uhss*) containing some of the substances needed to keep a body healthy

paralyze to make an animal or a person unable to move

pop art an art form in which the artists get their ideas from advertisements, brand names, and cartoons

process (*PROSS ess*) to treat food in a special way in order to preserve it

ration (*RASH uhn*) a limited allowance of something, such as food

recycle (*ree SYE kuhl*) to process used items, such as cans, so that they can be reused

reliable (*ri LYE uh buhl*) trustworthy

revolutionize (*rev uh LOO shuh nize*) to change something completely

spore (*SPOR*) a seed-like structure that can grow into a new living thing

starvation suffering or death from lack of food

surplus an amount greater than is used or needed

toxin (*TOK sin*) a poison made by a plant or an animal

trade card a collectable card put out by a company to advertise its products

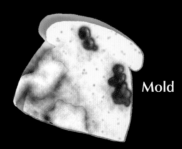

Mold

FIND OUT MORE

BOOKS

Jango-Cohen, Judith. *The History of Food.* Twenty-First Century Books, 2006.

Llewellyn, Claire. *Metal.* Franklin Watts, 2002.

MacGregor, Cynthia. *Recycling a Can.* Rosen Publishing Group, 2002.

Ridley, Sarah. *A Metal Can.* Gareth Stevens Publishing, 2007.

Strom, Laura Layton. *The Rock We Eat: Salt.* Scholastic Inc., 2008.

Tocci, Salvatore. *Aluminum.* Children's Press, 2005.

WEB SITES

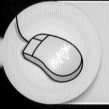

Go to the Web sites below to learn more about canning and recycling.

www.cancentral.com

www.westlerfoods.com/pdf/canning_process.pdf

www.recycleyourcans.org

www.planetpals.com/worldlywise.html

www.eia.doe.gov/kids/energyfacts/saving/recycling/solidwaste/
metals.html

INDEX

ABOUT THE AUTHOR

Maureen Mecozzi likes to cook (and eat) almost as much as she likes to write. "I used to raise my own chickens, grow vegetables, and keep bees," she says. She had to learn how to preserve food or else be swamped with whatever was in season. Maureen hopes her readers will want to learn more about the everyday items we take for granted, such as cans and bottles. "When you read, you explore new ideas," she says. "Those ideas might inspire you to think about things in a new way too."